Successful
Purchasing

in a week

Stephen Carter

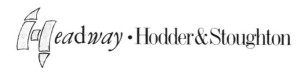

eadway · Hodder & Stoughton

British Library Cataloguing in Publication Data

A catalogue for this title is available from
the British Library

ISBN 0 340 627387

First published 1995
Impression number   10   9   8   7   6   5   4   3   2   1
Year   1999   1998   1997   1996   1995

Typeset by Multiplex Techniques Ltd, St Mary Cray, Kent.
Printed in Great Britain for Hodder & Stoughton Educational,
a division of Hodder Headline Plc, 338 Euston Road, London
NW1 3BH by St Edmundsbury Press, Bury St Edmunds,
Suffolk.

**the Institute
of Management**

F O U N D A T I O N

The Institute of Management (IM) is at the forefront of management development and best management practice. The Institute embraces all levels of management from students to chief executives. It provides a unique portfolio of services for all managers, enabling them to develop skills and achieve management excellence.

For information on the benefits of membership, please contact:

Department HS
Institute of Management
Cottingham Road
Corby
Northants NN17 1TT

Tel: 0536 204222
Fax: 0536 201651

This series is commissioned by the Institute of Management Foundation.

C O N T E N T S

Introduction		5
Sunday	Role and scope of purchasing	6
Monday	Objectives and strategy	16
Tuesday	Deciding what to buy	28
Wednesday	Selecting and managing suppliers	41
Thursday	Determining the price	56
Friday	Special purchases	69
Saturday	Performance measures and continuous improvement	80

The nature of purchasing and supply is changing fast as more and more people begin to recognise the enormous impact it can have on a company's ability to prosper in today's fiercely competitive markets.

This means that the skills, personal characteristics and objectives of a modern buyer are radically different from those of even a few years ago.

The aim of this book is to provide an easy-to-understand summary of the requirements of modern purchasing for buyers and all those involved in the buying process.

We shall build up our understanding by looking at different aspects of these requirements on each day of a week.

The steps to understanding purchasing:

Sunday	–	Role and scope
Monday	–	Objectives and strategy
Tuesday	–	Deciding what to buy
Wednesday	–	Selecting and managing suppliers
Thursday	–	Determining the price
Friday	–	Special purchases
Saturday	–	Performance measures

Role and scope of purchasing

Although most people will readily admit that they neither like nor are good at selling, everyone believes him or herself to be a good buyer. We all do it in our everyday life and have honed our skills over the years. These skills are easily transferred to business life – or so we think!

Today we look at the role and scope of purchasing and how and why they have changed over the last few years. In particular, we will see why purchasing is increasingly becoming a battleground for competitive advantage in the '90s and why the skills and strategies of buyers should not be taken for granted.

Although much of this section has a manufacturing perspective, the concepts are equally applicable to service and public organisations. We will look at the development of purchasing by considering:

- Changes in business affecting purchasing
- New pressures on purchasing
- The tasks of a buyer
- The role of suppliers
- The role of buyers

Changes in business affecting purchasing

Business over the last three decades has seen several major initiatives, the end result being a fundamental change in the way that purchasing operates.

The first was in the 1960s and 1970s when the marketing revolution took place. Up to that time, postwar shortages had meant that most people were conditioned to being happy to buy whatever was available. The marketing concept ended all that by tailoring a company's product or service to meet the specific need of individual market segments.

This resulted in much wider product ranges, ever shorter product life cycles and increasingly higher quality standards as consumers became more discerning. In turn, this meant that buyers had to find suppliers who could develop a wider range of materials and parts, shorten their development timescales and meet very stringent quality standards.

It is difficult to meet these customer needs at a profit using the traditional methods of manufacture developed for mass-market products. This led to a second wave of initiatives in the 1980s which centred on manufacturing. These included Just-in-Time (JIT) manufacture and total quality management (TQM), both of which address the people, process and product development issues that are directly under management's control.

However, although JIT and TQM go a long way towards aligning manufacturing operations with marketing strategy, their ultimate effectiveness is severely limited by the capability of suppliers to deliver defect-free materials and components in smaller, more frequent quantities at an affordable price.

A third change in business that affects purchasing is the way that organisations are restructuring into business units focused on customer requirements, with clear management responsibility and accountability.

This poses the question of where in the organisation purchasing should be placed. One argument is that buyers should be situated in the business units, as this makes them part of the team responsible for meeting the needs of a particular group of customers. They are then in a better position to meet customer requirements such as flexibility and responsiveness.

An alternative argument is that buyers should be in a centralised department where they can see the global needs of the organisation and consolidate purchases to achieve lower costs. A centralised department can also afford specialised skills which individual business units may not.

Whether centralised, decentralised or a mixture of the two, purchasing has become less independent, taking on a service role to its 'internal customers' in the business units.

New pressures on purchasing

In addition to these changes, other pressures have emerged over the last few years. They include:

- A move to 'get back to basics' in many companies, contracting out any operations that are not considered to be core activities. This increases the range, value and complexity of the products and services which they now purchase
- The recognition that 70% or more of a new product's cost is decided at the design stage and so early supplier involvement can contribute greatly to lower costs. This has implications for the way that suppliers are selected and managed
- Pressure from environmental lobbyists putting the accent on reuse, preservation and recycling. This

means that suppliers must develop existing products or buyers must search for new ones
- The recognition that as much as 65% of the cost of quality in your own manufacturing process is caused by the quality of items purchased from suppliers

The tasks of a buyer

Faced with this array of changes and pressures, what should be the tasks of a modern buyer?

Open most text books on purchasing and they will probably tell you that the task of a buyer is to obtain the right goods, at the right price, at the right time, in the right quantity and of the right quality. In other words, the traditional task of buyers centres around:

- Ensuring short-term supply
- Improving cost competitiveness
- Ensuring long-term supply
- Contributing to product innovation

Short-term availability is often the number one priority in the buying department, as failure in this area is very obvious to everyone, and can have severe financial repercussions if production is stopped as a result.

Once availability is assured, price reductions become the next priority. Buyers have long recognised that purchased components and raw materials account for anywhere between 50% and 80% of manufacturing costs. Add to this expenditure on services and capital items, and the scope for improving profits by reducing purchase prices is plain to see.

To achieve both these objectives, buyers often adopt confrontational approaches to supplier management that centre on:

- Bulk buying to get volume discounts and so keep unit costs down
- High stock levels to maintain availability and compensate for inadequate quality
- A large supplier base to create competitive pressure and provide alternatives for short-term supply
- No long-term commitment
- Investment in order processing and expediting systems to cope with the large number of purchase orders needed

Unfortunately, this can lead to:

- Long lead times
- Variable standards in supply and quality
- No supplier involvement in new product development, product or process improvement or cost reductions
- High support costs
- Little trust and cooperation

In other words, the opposite of what the purchasing department needs from its supplier base.

The role of suppliers

It is clear that a company needs the cooperation of its suppliers, particularly if it operates in fiercely competitive markets, where there is constant change and improvement in technology capability and customer expectations. The approaches to supplier management described earlier do not encourage them to enter into new ways of doing business.

For the key purchased items, the way forward is to introduce the concept of partnership sourcing. This entails both buying and supplying organisations forming a close, long-term relationship and working together to gain a commercial advantage which they can share. It works where both sides have a vested interest in the other's success. We will return to partnership sourcing later in the week but for now the key issues are:

- The recognition that the lowest unit purchase price may not give the lowest overall cost
- Suppliers need the confidence of long-term business with us in order to invest time and money in making the improvements that we want
- A commitment to eliminate waste in all its forms in the supply relationship
- Balancing the time commitment needed to make the partnership work with the risk from having a single source of supply

The role of buyers

It should be clear by now that the requirements of a modern purchasing department require a different approach from buyers to that which has been successful in the past.

The traditional role of a buyer has been to react to a purchase request from a user by finding a supply source (often by getting three or four competitive bids), negotiating the terms of the purchase, and handling the administration of the purchase by raising a purchase order, which can be subsequently matched with a goods received note, an invoice and the original requisition note.

Today the buyer's role is much wider. Being world class is more about the total company effort in meeting customer needs at a profit, rather than in achieving excellence in individual functional departments.

A key element in achieving this is the integration of the supply chain. The role of the buyer is becoming increasingly one of managing the interface between the supply market and his own company. This means that the buyer is involved much earlier in the buying process, and is required to monitor supply markets, anticipate trends, and manage suppliers to achieve common aims of better service at lower cost.

Achieving all of these tasks requires specific skills from a buyer. In some cases these will be new skills. They include:

- Coaching and mentoring skills to bring out the best in your suppliers
- Communication and persuasion skills to convey your vision, goals and plans
- Psychology skills to enable you to motivate the different players in your game plan
- Financial analysis skills to identify the true costs of your supply channels
- Market research skills to monitor your supply markets regularly

- Strategy skills so that your goals and objectives mesh with those of the rest of the organisation

Summary

To summarise what we have learned today:

- Fundamental changes in business, such as marketing and TQM, have created the need for a new approach to purchasing
- This has led to new tasks for buyers, in particular the need to focus on more than just price
- The new approach also requires suppliers to adopt a new role, in many cases forming strategic partnerships with their key customers
- Which, in turn, means that buyers have to play a new role of supplier manager

Objectives and strategy

In this chapter, we will build on the concepts introduced yesterday, and describe effective strategies for managing different categories of purchase. The way we will do this is to use an approach based on the product portfolio matrix idea developed by Peter Kraljic.

The idea behind the matrix is that management needs to have a supply strategy for its purchases if it is to meet the demands of its end market. This is particularly true when there is a risk of a long-term scarcity due to technological change or economic and political instability around the world. However, not all purchases warrant the investment of time and effort needed to develop and implement a strategy. Some form of prioritisation is needed.

The portfolio matrix approach achieves this prioritisation by considering two factors for each purchase: its importance to your company, and the complexity of the supply market for that item.

Importance of purchased items

The first step in the approach is to rank purchased items in order of their importance to your company. There are many factors which can make an item important. Some of these are shown below:

- The annual spend on the purchased item
- If the item is used to make products which may be few in number but which together contribute a major part of our sales and profit
- If the item is used to make a large number of our products
- If the item is used on a bottleneck resource where failure in availability or quality can potentially stop the entire factory's output
- If the item is used in new products which are vital to the future growth of the company
- Where the cost of non-availability is high

If we have a wide range of purchases, then analysing each one in terms of all these factors may be somewhat daunting. For simplicity, we can use the annual spend on the product expressed as a percentage of the total annual spend on all purchases as a measure of its importance. Further, we can make an arbitrary assumption that if the resulting percentage is less than one, then the item has low importance, and if it is greater than one, its importance is high.

Supply complexity

We now need to analyse the supply complexity of each of these products. We need to ask ourselves the following questions for each of our supply markets.

- Is the product or service in scarce supply?
- Is the pace of technological change high?
- Is it impossible to use an alternative product or service?
- Are the barriers for a new supplier to enter the market high?
- Are the logistics costs of acquiring the product or service high?

The more 'yes' answers given, the more complex the supply market is likely to be.

Another aspect of supply complexity is that of supply risk. There are many types of risk but the one which causes buyers the most concern is the risk of non-availability. Different supply markets will have different degrees of risk attached to them.

For example, if we buy nuts and bolts to a widely used specification, such as a British Standard, and there are many distributors of these items offering off-the-shelf availability, all within easy geographical reach, then the supply risk is low.

On the other hand, if we buy a manufactured part from a supplier who has a six-month lead time, and the supplier is the only one approved by your quality engineers, then the supply risk is high.

A simple way to assess supply complexity for a 'first cut' view is to look at the number of suppliers who are both willing and able to supply that product. We may not necessarily buy from all of these suppliers at present. In the main, if there are fewer than five such suppliers, the associated risk and complexity is high and if there are more than five, the supply risk and complexity can be considered to be low.

The matrix

We are now in a position to draw up a portfolio matrix for our purchases. As the example below shows, there are four quadrants to the matrix, determined by whether their importance and supply complexity is high or low.

	Importance	
	Low	*High*
Low	**Non-critical** Handle efficiently	**Leverage** Exploit market potential
High	**Bottleneck** Ensure supply	**Strategic** Cooperate

Complexity

Non-critical items

These are products or services which are necessary for the smooth running of a company but which in themselves do not represent a major supply risk or have a major impact on the business. The supply risk is low because there are more than five potential suppliers in the market-place who are both willing and able to supply. The impact is low because they represent less than 1% of the total annual purchase spend of the company.

The Pareto effect, which states that 80% of purchased items typically account for 20% of the total spend, means that this category usually has a very large number of small value items. In turn, this means that a buyer can spend a large percentage of his or her time in procuring these items if the same purchasing process is used for everything. In many companies, it is still the practice to obtain three or more quotes before placing an order every time a purchase need is triggered.

The strategy for non-critical items should be to make the purchasing process as efficient as possible. This may mean negotiating contracts with single sources which are reviewed every year, or every other year, and placing blanket orders which cover all the items bought from that supplier. Users then call-in their requirements by telephone, fax or EDI.

This limits a buyer's involvement to yearly renegotiation of the contract, unless there are problems in delivery or quality during the year. The resulting savings in a buyer's time can be as high as 40%, time which can then be put to use on more value-adding activities.

Other key activities for this category are product standardisation and order volume optimisation. Product standardisation means using as small a range of products as possible to serve the needs of all users. For example, one company the author knows used to buy 73 different types of glue for its packaging operation. Close examination of the real needs of the users allowed this to be reduced to just seven different types. The larger quantities of these seven also meant that the buyer was able to obtain significant price reductions.

Order volume optimisation means that when we reorder a product from a supplier, we should look to see if any other products bought from that supplier may need to be ordered soon. If so, by ordering them all at the same time, we may be able to make savings on costs such as transport, which more than outweigh any short-term increased inventory holding costs.

Information requirements for the non-critical category of purchases consist of a good overview of the supply markets and good short-term forecasting of requirements. In large purchasing departments these products are generally sourced by junior buyers.

Leverage items

With leverage items, purchasers generally have significant bargaining power with suppliers because the value of purchases is large, and there is a lot of competition in the market-place due to the large number of potential suppliers.

This bargaining power can be exploited by using spot buying to get the lowest prices, or by working with suppliers on value analysis and cost-reduction projects. If we believe that market prices are going to increase and stay there for a while, we may use our leverage to negotiate longer-term contracts at today's lower prices.

Leverage items require us to have systems in place which give good market and supplier information and allow us to plan our short- and medium-term demands as well as to forecast price movements. These items are generally the responsibility of senior buying personnel.

Bottleneck items

These items are generally bad news as far as a buyer is concerned. They usually arise due to patents, the need to certify suppliers or from a specialised technology which is not universally used. There is a potential supply risk because there are few suppliers available, and leverage with the supplier is small because the value of purchases is relatively low.

In the short term, our tactics should be to secure supply by negotiating favourable contracts or investing in inventory. Longer term, we, and our colleagues in engineering, design and manufacturing, should seek to find alternative products with a wider potential supply base.

We will need good medium- to long-term forecasts of demand and good market intelligence. In larger organisations, bottleneck items are the responsibility of higher level management such as the purchasing head.

Strategic items
The key tasks for managing this group of products are:

- Make or buy decision-making
- Accurate demand forecasting
- Detailed market research
- Development of long-term supply relationships
- Contingency planning and risk analysis

We will need quite detailed information on supply markets, long-term supply and demand trends, and industry cost curves. The strategic impact that these products can have on our business means that decisions are usually made at a very high level in the organisation, such as by the Purchasing Director.

The strategy and tactics that we select largely depends on the relative strengths of the buyer and the supplier. These need to be analysed very carefully, as explained in the next section.

Supply market analysis

The next step for the products we have classified as strategic is to assess the supply market systematically in terms of the relative strengths of existing suppliers, and then to compare it with a similar analysis of our own bargaining strength. Factors which determine a supplier's strength are:

- Market size versus the supplier's capacity
- Market growth versus the supplier's capacity growth
- Supplier's capacity utilisation
- Profitability of the supplier
- Supplier's cost and price structure
- Level at which the supplier breaks even
- Uniqueness of the product and the stability of the technology used
- Entry barriers, either 'know how' or capital, for companies wishing to enter the market

On the other hand, factors which make a buyer strong include:

- Purchase volume versus capacity of main suppliers
- Demand growth versus capacity growth
- Capacity utilisation of main suppliers
- Market share compared to main competition
- Profitability of main products
- Own production capability for making the purchased product
- Cost and price structure

One way to measure the relative strengths is to use a scoring system for each of the factors mentioned. This can be a rating from, say, 1 to 5. The total scored is then an indication of strength. For example:

- less than 10 = low strength
- 11 to 20   = medium strength
- more than 20 = high strength

We can then compare our bargaining position with each of our suppliers' using the following matrix.

		Low	Medium	High
Buyers strength	*High*	Exploit	Exploit	Balance
	Medium	Exploit	Balance	Diversify
	Low	Balance	Diversify	Diversify
		Low	*Medium*	*High*

Supplier strength

This comparison will show us which of three basic strategic thrusts are available to us. For items where we dominate the market and the supplier's strength is low to medium, we should try to exploit our advantage by negotiating favourable prices and contract terms. Even so, we should be careful not to jeopardise long-term relationships, or to provoke counter measures which may in the end prove costly.

Where suppliers are very much stronger than us, we need to adopt a more defensive strategy. This means taking steps to ensure supply in the short term, for example, by building up strategic stocks, whilst we search for substitute products. In other words, diversifying from our current product.

If the comparison shows that there is a balance of strength with our suppliers, we need to adopt a strategy which is not too defensive and costly, but which at the same time is not overly aggressive and damaging to supplier relationships.

Summary

Today we have looked at a way to build a strategy for procuring goods and services which allows us to formulate and prioritise plans for managing our supply base. The key steps are:

- Rank all purchases in terms of their importance to our company
- Assess the complexity of the market-place for these purchases paying particular attention to supply risk
- Based on their importance and supply complexity, decide whether each purchase is non-critical, bottleneck, leverage or strategic and adopt the appropriate strategy and tactics
- For the strategic items, compare our bargaining strength with our suppliers' and decide whether to exploit our position, diversify from that product or follow a balanced strategy

Deciding what to buy

In deciding what we have to buy, there are three things that we need to determine.

The first question we have to answer is whether we should buy the goods from external sources or make it ourselves. This question should also be asked of services which we propose contracting out, and is called a 'make or buy' decision.

Second, we need to prepare some kind of description of the items that we do have to purchase from suppliers. This is called a specification and is a key statement in ensuring that suppliers understand and deliver exactly what we need.

The third item that we have then to consider, is how to decide when to purchase and in what quantity. This is not always as easy and straightforward as it appears.

Make or buy decisions

One of the roles of the buyer is to review all potential
sources of supply, and to select suppliers who will give the
lowest overall cost. Too often, we think of this activity
purely in terms of external suppliers. However, for some
goods or services, our own company may be capable of
providing what we want. The comparison between using
our own company as a supplier and using a third party is
called a make or buy decision.

The factors which shape the make or buy decision are:

1 The relative costs of making or buying the item or
   service
2 The capacity situation of the company
3 The future supply market

Relative costs
The easiest way to explain the relative cost side of the make
or buy equation is to look at a simple example. Suppose our
accountant has estimated the cost per unit of our company
producing a part and it looks like this:

	£
Direct material	15
Direct labour	5
Variable overhead	2
Fixed overhead	6
Total cost	28

We discover from our supply market research that the same item can be bought on the open market for £25. Should we make it or buy it?

On the face of it, we should buy it because to do so appears to be £3 cheaper. However, if we think about the 'before' and 'after' situations of producing it ourselves, we get a different picture.

	If we make the part	If we don't make the part
	£	£
Direct material	15	0
Direct labour	5	0
Variable overhead	2	0
Fixed costs	6	6
Total cost	28	6

The difference between making the part ourselves and not making it ourselves is really £22. This is because the fixed costs of production are with us whether we make anything or not. The incremental cost to us is really the direct variable costs and these should be the only ones considered. On this basis, it is cheaper to make the part ourselves than to buy it from a supplier.

Capacity considerations

This is all very well if we have sufficient capacity to make the volume of the part that we want. What if we don't have sufficient capacity? In that case, we have to calculate what contribution to fixed overheads and profit we would have earned if we hadn't been making this new part. This then becomes an 'opportunity cost' which we must include in the overall cost calculation.

Future supply conditions

In addition to the quantitative aspects of calculating the relative costs of making or buying the part, there are other considerations which are more qualitative and subjective.

For example, if we decide to source the part or service with an external supplier, is the future supply market likely to be reliable? Our analyses from our portfolio matrix will help in this but we will need market research systems to help continually review the situation.

What is the likely stability of prices in the future? Our decision to source the part externally has been made on the basis of current prices. Will prices increase faster than internal manufacturing costs and will this change the decision? Sensitivity analyses at the decision-making stage will help us to determine the price range in which the decision remains the correct one.

Purchase descriptions

A description of what the user wants has to be relayed to suppliers often via the purchasing department. Unless there is a way of making sure that the message of what is wanted is not distorted, there is a risk that suppliers will misinterpret our requirements.

One mechanism for providing clear and unambiguous messages of what is required, is the purchase specification. There are three basic types of specification:

- Commercial
- Design
- Performance

Commercial specifications
These are specifications produced by a national or governing body such as the British Standards Institute. They set out standards for the quality of materials used, the quality of workmanship involved in production, as well as for such items as critical dimensions, chemical composition and allowable tolerances.

Nuts, bolts and chemicals are the kind of items often covered by a commercial specification. They are all items with a wide application, and so manufacturers can plan production with the confidence that there will be a large demand. This confidence allows them to have long production runs which give them high efficiencies and low costs. These costs can then be passed on in the form of low prices, one reason for specifying a product with a commercial specification whenever possible.

Design specifications

If the cost of the standard item is unacceptable, or if there is a supply risk because the product is protected by patent or copyright, it may be worthwhile developing our own specification in order to increase the potential supply base.

The danger in doing this is that we may produce a specification that is too detailed. This may incur unnecessary cost because it does not allow suppliers to use their expertise in producing it. It may also mean that the buyer unintentionally assumes all responsibility for the performance of the purchased part. For example, if we specify that a dimension has to have a tolerance of +/−0.01 cm when, in fact, it should be +/−0.005 cm then the responsibility is ours.

Performance specifications

Performance specifications avoid the drawbacks of design specifications by specifying in detail the performance required, but not the method of achieving that performance. In this way, suppliers are free to choose the materials they use and the manufacturing process they employ. Giving suppliers this leeway should result in lower costs because we are allowing them to use their expertise in producing the item.

When to buy

The timing of the purchase decision for many one-off purchases such as office equipment, training and cars is relatively straightforward. If a budget has been agreed with management, and the finance is available, then the timing of the purchase is dictated by the user's need for the purchased item.

The timing of the purchase decision for repeat purchases, such as direct production materials and consumables, is more complicated. Factors which complicate the decision-making process are:

- The quantity we currently possess compared with the quantity we need in the near future
- The lead time between issuing an order to a supplier and receiving the goods
- Any minimum order quantities for purchases from the supplier
- The requirements for other products we buy from the same supplier which it may be desirable to order at the same time to reduce transport costs

Holding stocks

In many companies these considerations often result in the decision to keep some stock of the item to ensure availability when needed. The question then is, how much stock should be kept?

The answer to this lies in the diagram below which shows the fundamentals of a stock system, commonly referred to as a reorder point system. In this system, stock eventually reaches a level called the reorder point (ROP) at which an order is issued to the supplier. The standard supply lead time (L) is the usual time taken between the order being issued and the buyer receiving the goods.

During this lead time, the buying company uses, on average, D units of the part. The risk to the buying company is that usage for the part will be greater than D during the lead time and that they will, therefore, run out before the order arrives. As a result, it is common practice to keep a safety stock (S) which will cater for some of this above-average usage. The average amount in stock is the safety stock plus half the reorder quantity (Q).

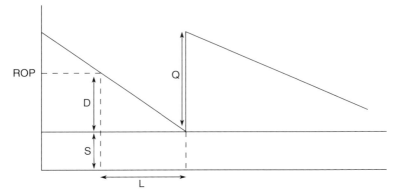

Timing decisions for items controlled by a reorder point system are then made semi-automatically, in that the system will recommend that an order be placed when the current on-hand stock falls below the reorder point. Buyers should review these suggestions and amend as necessary, based on their knowledge of current supplier performance and their own company's needs.

Improving stock performance

Once the reorder report system for placing orders with suppliers is working efficiently, we can turn our attention to improving its performance. There are three things we can do to reduce the amount of stock needed for a given level of availability.

Improving forecasts
The more accurate we can get our forecast, the less safety stock we will need to carry to buffer production from uncertainties in requirements.

The first step is to choose an appropriate statistical method for our forecasting. Most forecasting methods are based on the assumption that demand for a product in the immediate future will bear some kind of relationship to that shown in the past. A simple way of forecasting based on this assumption is to use a 'moving average'. More sophisticated systems using exponential smoothing techniques will give a more robust result, but are correspondingly more difficult to use and interpret.

Reducing supplier lead times
Reducing supplier lead times has two benefits for stock holding. The first is that the shorter the lead time, the less safety stock we need to hold to cover for uncertainties in demand during the lead time.

The second benefit is that, the shorter the lead time, the shorter the horizon over which we need to forecast. This should mean that our forecasts are more accurate, which in turn means that we need to hold less stock.

Reducing purchase quantities
The second component of stock holding is the purchase quantity. Any quantity which is greater than our immediate requirements goes into stock. The greater the quantity purchased at any one time, the more that will have to be stored for future use, and the greater the average stock holding.

The traditional way to calculate the 'correct' quantity to purchase, is to use the economic order quantity formula.

The major problem with this, is that it accepts the need for costs and merely trades one type of cost for another. A much better approach is to work with suppliers to find ways of making it cost-effective to deliver a quantity of just one, if that is all that is required.

Materials requirements planning

Reorder point systems, such as the one just described, are fine for products which have what is called 'independent demand'. In other words, the sale or usage of that product is not determined by the sale or usage of another product.

However, this is not generally the case for materials or products used in a manufacturing process. For example, a manufacturer of bicycles knows that for every bicycle he makes he will need two wheels. The demand for wheels is determined by the number of bicycles he plans to make. Wheels are then said to have dependent demand.

WHERE'S THE SPARE WHEEL?

The problem in using reorder point systems for dependent demand items is that the probability of having all the components we need when we need them falls with the increase in the number of components used. Unless you are prepared to hold very high levels of stock of components, which is expensive, you may not be able to meet all manufacturing's requirements.

A more effective way of planning purchases to meet manufacturing's needs is to use a system called 'materials requirements planning' or 'mrp'. This uses manufacturing's master production schedule, or MPS, as its starting point. The MPS identifies the products and their quantities which will be manufactured in each week or month for the next six to 12 months.

The MPS is then 'exploded' into a list of all the components that will be needed to manufacture the MPS requirements and the dates on which they will be used. Knowing the supply lead times for the components allows buyers to schedule purchases from suppliers so that the correct quantities are received by the required date.

The result is that the buyer can meet the demand from his manufacturing department, and at the same time keep little or no stock of his own.

Just in Time supply

Another book in this series looks at Just in Time manufacture and the dramatic effect it can have on a company's performance. The next logical step is to use the JIT philosophy to schedule purchases with suppliers.

The target is to develop a network of suppliers who can consistently deliver quantities which exactly match our immediate production requirements, at the time when we need them (not early or late) whilst meeting our quality standards every time. This will allow us to reduce our stock holding dramatically, and at the same time be more responsive to our customers' needs.

Summary

We have spent today looking at ways of deciding what items we should buy from outside our organisation, and of methods for deciding when to buy.

The first consideration was whether we could provide the item or service more economically from within our own organisation. This led us to look at make or buy decisions, and at how to calculate the relevant costs.

We next looked at the importance of product descriptions in making sure that the supplier knows exactly what we want, and that we are buying the most cost-effective means of meeting our needs.

We then looked at methods for deciding when to buy. These were:

- Stock holding systems which trigger an order when a certain stock level is reached
- Materials requirement planning systems which allow us to meet requirements with less stock by forecasting demand accurately
- Just in Time systems which trigger supplies on very short lead times to meet immediate requirements

Selecting and managing suppliers

The key to achieving our purchasing objectives of service at
least cost is the way in which we select, manage and
develop our suppliers. The major tasks for buyers in doing
this effectively are:

- Researching and monitoring both current and
  potential sources of supply
- Addressing the strategic and tactical issues in
  selecting suppliers
- Coordinating the inputs from the rest of the
  organisation in supplier selection
- Developing and controlling a plan to manage
  suppliers

Researching the supply base

There are many information sources available to buyers
these days which enable them to identify potential suppliers
of a product or service. A few of the most commonly used
sources are:

- Our own company's database of current and past
  suppliers
- Trade directories such as Kompass, Kelly's and
  Yellow Pages
- Trade press

- Suppliers themselves – either visits from the salesforce or other supplier initiatives such as direct mail shots
- Exhibitions and conferences
- Chambers of Commerce
- The trade section of Foreign Embassies for information on global sources

From these, we will be able to draw up a list of potential suppliers. However, we will also need to monitor our key markets continually for trends and events which may have an impact on our initial choice of supplier or even trigger the need to look for new suppliers.

In addition to the sources of information on current and potential suppliers, other sources of information which are useful for monitoring supply markets include:

- Company annual reports
- Market research firms such as Mintel who often undertake research for themselves which they make available to others at a reasonable price
- Suppliers' salesforces
- Our own employees
- Supplier advertising in the press, for example, recruitment advertising can give an indication of the supplier's expansion plans

Strategic and tactical issues

Before final selection of a supplier, there are several strategic and tactical issues which we need to agree with our management team.

Early supplier involvement
The experience of many companies has been that involving suppliers at an early stage in the development of their products can produce significant advantages. The areas in which suppliers can help us include:

- Setting specifications
- Agreeing tolerances
- Suggesting opportunities for standardisation
- Process and assembly improvements
- Packaging
- Inventory management
- Transportation

Colleagues need to agree to, and be aware of early supplier involvement because we need the suppliers' input before the design of a new product is frozen. Many companies only think about suppliers after the design has been set.

Early supplier involvement is an approach which is usually appropriate for certain products within the strategic and leverage areas of the product portfolio.

Single or multi-source?
Whether to have a policy of using a single or using two or more sources for added security is a thorny issue for many companies, but there is no clear cut reason to opt for one choice or the other.

In general, our strategy towards single or multi-sourcing is determined by a product's position in our portfolio. Non-critical parts should be single sourced, as the cost of administering a large supply base usually outweighs any of the benefits of multi-sourcing.

Leverage products can be a mixture of single and multi-sourced depending on whether we are using our leverage in these markets to secure long-term supply at advantageous prices, or are aiming to get low average prices from spot buying.

For bottleneck products, we should endeavour in the short term to secure supply. This may mean placing contracts with more than one supplier, if more than one is available, or negotiating a contract on favourable terms with just one supplier.

The same considerations apply to strategic products as for bottleneck products. Sharing our requirements on, say, a 60/40 basis with two suppliers may reduce our supply risk. This is particularly true if the balance of negotiating power lies with us.

Share of business

Buyers should always look to improve their negotiating position with suppliers. One way of doing this is to increase the volume of trade placed with them. The danger with this approach is that it can result in our business accounting for a very high percentage of their output. If we then decide to switch suppliers, it can have a devastating impact on the original company, even to the point of putting it out of business.

This is a moral dilemma that few companies would consciously wish to find themselves in. Indeed, many of the larger companies now have a policy of not taking more than, say, 30% of any supplier's output. However, adopting such a policy can mean that we have to dual or multi-source some products.

Local, national or global sourcing?

With modern communications and transport, it is now much easier to source products from further afield. One decision we will have to take is whether to source a product locally, nationally or even internationally. The advantages of local sourcing are:

- Better cooperation because it is easier to visit each other and sort out problems or attack opportunities
- Transport is a small part of the overall lead time for procurement and so stocks can be reduced, in fact this is a prerequisite of JIT supply
- Emergency orders are more easily met
- It helps to support the local community and so increases the company's public image

The advantages of buying nationally come from the fact that national suppliers tend to be bigger than local suppliers. This means that:

- Economies of scale get passed on to us in the form of lower prices
- They may be able to offer better technical assistance
- They may be able to meet any fluctuations in demand better because of their larger capacity
- Shortages are less likely to occur

The major reason that many companies now look to world markets for key purchases is lower prices. This price difference can more than offset the increased cost of sourcing overseas. However, there are potentially significant risks attached to overseas sourcing. These include:

- The length of the supply line which makes it difficult for suppliers to react to changes in requirements
- Increased inventory to safeguard availability given that lead times tend to be longer and more variable, particularly if the goods are transported by sea
- Exposure to currency fluctuations

Manufacturer or distributor
In some instances, we may have the option of sourcing products with either the manufacturer or one of its authorised distributors. An advantage of sourcing directly with the manufacturer is that we cut out the middle man and so should pay less.

On the other hand, distributors may offer a service which the manufacturer is not willing to provide, such as technical support and after-sales service. This is increasingly a factor when buying, for example, personal computers and peripheral equipment.

Also, distributors often deal in product lines from more than one manufacturer. We may find that we can concentrate our purchases with one distributor and use the leverage to get lower overall prices. Office stationery is one example where it can make sense to deal with a distributor rather than the individual manufacturers.

Selecting suppliers

Many departments within the company will have an interest in which suppliers are chosen. Each will have a different view on what makes a supplier a good one. Some of these views will be qualitative, others will be quantitative. Our task is to channel these different views into a coherent and consistent method for selecting suppliers that produces the best supplier base to meet our company's objectives.

The type of supplier evaluation we need to carry out depends on the nature of the product we are buying. We should use only a basic form of evaluation on products in the non-critical quadrant of our product portfolio in order to minimise the cost of evaluation. Items in the bottleneck and strategic quadrants need a more rigorous approach and it pays to make this evaluation a team effort. Suppliers of leverage products may or may not be given a rigorous evaluation depending on our strategy towards them.

Preliminary evaluation
We can do this with a mixture of desk research and a mail shot to potential suppliers asking for information. The information we need to gather includes:

- Product range
- Production capacity, both in total and current utilisation
- Quality standards achieved, such as BS 5750 (ISO 9000)
- Financial performance
- Credit rating, such as that awarded by Dun and Bradstreet
- Customer referrals

Follow-up evaluation
Now that we have a smaller list of potential suppliers, the next step is to investigate them in more detail. This is usually done by our team visiting their premises and carrying out an audit of their activities. The audit should cover their:

- Financial stability
- Ability to do the work
- Capacity to do the work
- Understanding of our needs

In addition, we need to assess them in terms of what they are like to deal with as people. This is important as many problems and opportunities depend on the way that we all work together as a team.

We will need to use a standard document in making this assessment so that the team is consistent in the way that it evaluates different companies. It will also aid later comparisons between competing suppliers. A simple example is shown on the next page. In practice, we may need to go much deeper than this.

We should also bear in mind when conducting these visits that it is an opportunity for us to sell our own company to the supplier. This can be important if we are very much smaller than the supplier, and we need to ensure the supply of products in the strategic or bottleneck areas.

Supplier Evaluation Form

Rate the supplier on a scale of 0 to 5 for each of the categories below. The evaluation ratings should be interpreted as follows:

1 = poor and could not be improved in the short term
2 = poor but could be improved with considerable effort
3 = meets the standard required in most aspects
4 = meets the standard required in all respects
5 = exceeds the standard in all respects

Supplier attitude
- Willingness to respond to our needs
- Ability to respond to our needs
- Quality of consultation on new product development
- Quality of market information supplied
- Initiatives in cost reduction measures

Technical ability
- Technical competence
- Process capability
- Process control

Commercial
- Lead time
- Supplier location
- Delivery frequency
- Minimum order quantities
- % order schedules filled on time
- Supply risk
- Purchase price

Financial
- Credit terms
- Credit rating
- Key financial ratios

Managing and developing suppliers

A well-motivated and responsive supplier base is a valuable asset to any company. This is particularly true in high technology industries or where there is potential for scarcity of key raw materials.

Such a supplier base is achieved by developing goodwill through the way that we manage and develop our suppliers. It means being completely open, impartial and fair at all times. If achieved, goodwill can encourage suppliers to invest time and effort in understanding our business and its problems, and to work with us to find solutions.

The potential for improving company performance in this way is so great that many companies have decided to form partnerships with their key suppliers. This is being encouraged in the UK by the formation of Partnership Sourcing Ltd., a project which is jointly sponsored by the Department of Trade and Industry and the Confederation of British Industry. The key steps to achieving partnerships are as follows:

Deciding on the markets and products
The first step is to review company strategy. This will help us to decide on the sort of suppliers we will need in order to achieve our corporate objectives concerning company size, new products and key markets. Using the portfolio matrix analysis we performed earlier in the week, we can identify the strategic products which would benefit from partnership sourcing. We can then develop an action plan based on this strategic review of products and markets to put forward to the rest of our organisation.

Selling the idea

As with any major initiative, support from top management is vital. The action plan we developed from our strategic analysis will help us to communicate the benefits to be gained as a result of improved quality and service and a reduction in total cost.

We also need to sell the concept to other departments in our own company. Many of these will be able either to help or obstruct our efforts to introduce partnership sourcing. For example, accounts need to pay suppliers on time and production needs to communicate changes in their plans which affect suppliers.

Finally, we need to sell the idea to our key suppliers. We will need to stress the benefits to them of: stability due to long-term contracts; lower costs from such areas as better planning and design, simplified logistics and cooperative cost reduction projects; and strategic advantages, such as access to our technology, shared problem-solving and management input.

Choosing our first partners

First, we need to define the parameters for selecting partners. These include many of the factors on our supplier evaluation form. We can then review our current suppliers' performance against these parameters for evidence that they could be good partners.

Define what we both want from the partnership

We will need to develop a style of working together with which both sides feel comfortable. Much of this is intangible and cannot be measured, covering things like trust,

commitment, flexibility, teamwork and persistence.
Practical tools to help foster the working relationship
include the use of continuous improvement teams, open-
book accounting and continuous assessment.

If partnerships are to work, they must have tangible
objectives on which both sides are agreed. These must be
defined at the start of the partnership and targets and plans
set for their accomplishment. They include topics such as:

- Total costs
- Total quality management
- Zero defects
- Joint research and development
- Faster time to market
- JIT deliveries

Making the partnership work
Partnerships will not work by themselves. We must have a
process for monitoring progress, resolving problems as they

occur, and communicating the results so as to build commitment and enthusiasm for the project. The way to do this is to:

- Set up a joint review team which meets regularly. This team is responsible for monitoring progress and making sure the project meets it deadlines. It is also responsible for resourcing problem-solving teams to attack the major issues
- Implement systems for monitoring and measuring progress. These should measure progress to agreed targets on criteria such as on-time deliveries, lead times, service levels and failure rates
- Build the relationship through activities such as sharing business plans, joint research and development, and sharing technology

Summary

Today, we have concentrated on how to select and manage suppliers for peak performance. The key steps are:

- Thorough research of potential sources of supply
- Addressing the strategic and tactical issues around the sort of supply base required
- Selection of suppliers using a rigorous evaluation process which allows different suppliers to be compared fairly
- For key suppliers, the implementation of a supply partnership agreement

Determining the price

This is perhaps the most crucial aspect of purchasing. Any reduction in the purchase price paid will show in the accounts of the company as an equal increase in profits. Hence the pressure brought to bear on buyers to get the lowest price possible.

No one would argue against this in principle. However, there are other costs to bear in mind when purchasing goods and services. Typical sources of additional cost for many companies include:

- Purchasing systems for generating purchase requisitions, orders, acknowledgements and processing supplier invoices
- Material handling costs for unloading, storing and moving goods which are not required immediately
- Checking the supplier by counting goods received, issuing receiving reports, inspecting the quality of goods received and sorting the good ones from the bad ones
- Poor quality resulting in scrap, rework or return transportation to the supplier

The buyer's task is to reduce the overall cost, not just the purchase price.

Purchase price

Getting the right price can mean the difference between success and failure for many companies. What constitutes the right price can change over time and so our approach to pricing must be continually reviewed. An understanding of the factors which contribute to this decision-making process is vital.

Cost behaviour
In the long run, all companies must recover all their costs if they are to stay in business. There are three major categories of cost:

- Variable costs: these are costs which vary with the volume of product or service provided. For example, raw materials in a manufacturing company are a variable cost. If production is increased, the cost of raw materials will increase in direct proportion to the increased volume of product produced. Equally, if production is reduced, raw material costs will reduce in proportion
- Fixed costs: these are costs which have to be paid even if production is zero. Labour costs in a service organisation are a good example of a fixed cost as is the cost of rent in a manufacturing company. Fixed costs tend to vary with time rather than volume of production, within certain limits
- Semi-variable costs: some costs are neither purely variable or purely fixed. An example of this is maintenance costs. This consists of planned maintenance, the fixed element, which is undertaken no matter what the level of production activity and unplanned maintenance, such as repairs, which varies in proportion to the level of production

However, in the short term, companies may be prepared to accept a price which just recovers the variable element of their costs. A knowledge of costs and cost behaviour for companies in your supply market can give you an edge in negotiations.

A useful tool for analysing company costs is break-even analysis. This is a chart which shows how the costs of a company change with different volumes of output. The diagram overleaf shows just such an analysis. One can be constructed for any supplier by performing these steps:

1   On a sheet of paper, draw a horizontal line to represent the range of output of the company from 0 to 100%.

2   Take the total sales value (£20m in our example) from the firm's latest annual accounts and plot this value on the vertical axis of the graph. On the horizontal axis plot the normal operating output of the company for the period covered by the annual accounts (in our example, this is 80%). It is unlikely that we will be able to get an accurate figure for this, unless our supplier tells us. We will need to use our judgement and experience from visiting the supplier to gauge what this is likely to be. Mark on the graph where these two values intersect.

3   Draw a straight line from 0 to the point just plotted, and extend it to the limit of the chart (i.e. to 100%).

4   Again from the annual accounts, take the value of fixed costs and locate this on the vertical axis. Starting from this point, draw a horizontal line across the graph.

5   Take the total cost (in our example £15m) from the annual accounts and mark where this value intersects with the operating level we used previously (i.e. 80%).

6   Draw a line between the start of the fixed cost line and this point and extend it to the limit of the graph.

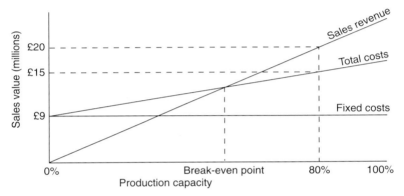

The break-even point is the point at which the total cost line intersects the total sales line. The corresponding value on the horizontal axis is the capacity at which the company must operate in order to break even. Operating at a level above this, the company makes a profit. Below it, the company makes a loss.

It must be stressed that the accuracy of this approach is dependent on the accuracy of the data used to construct it. The cost data available to buyers from published sources, such as annual accounts, will be aggregate data for the company as a whole and not for a particular product. Consequently, the approach works best in process industries where companies tend to have small product ranges. Nevertheless, it is a useful source of information to use with suppliers in negotiations.

Suppliers' pricing behaviour

Different companies will have different priorities and strategies when it comes to pricing their product range. A knowledge of this enables the enterprising buyer to use his or her market and cost knowledge to best effect when negotiating prices.

For a start, most companies do not sell just one product, but a range of products. They will not necessarily expect to make the same profit margin on all. Indeed, if they do price products in such a way that all products earn the same margin, then the most efficiently produced products will be overpriced. This can be used as a lever to obtain reductions on some items in the range.

Similarly, many companies will not expect all customers to earn them the same level of profit. We should use our leverage to make sure that our company is one of the low margin customers.

Modifying the price

Most companies modify their prices to encourage certain types of behaviour. For example, a discount may be given for early payment. This reduces the supplier's credit collection costs and potential bad debt costs, as well as improving liquidity.

A quantity discount for buying a large volume is another way that a supplier can reduce the costs involved in selling, storing inventory and transportation.

Functional discounts (also called trade discounts) are given to customers who, in return, perform some service in the supply channel, such as selling, storing or record keeping.

Seasonal discounts are sometimes given in situations where demand for a product varies with the time of year. By offering a lower price out of season, sales volume can be increased and so keep production at a more constant level.

Pricing analysis

It is clear that with all these factors potentially influencing the price of a product, we must perform some kind of price analysis for every purchase made. There are four tools which we can use as an aid in this analysis:

- Competitive bidding
- Comparison with market prices
- Comparison with historical prices
- Target pricing

Competitive bidding
This form of price comparison is normally used in situations where the following six conditions exist.

1   The value of the purchase is high enough to justify the cost involved for both the buyer and the seller in preparing and analysing the invitation to tender and the subsequent bid.

2   The specification of the purchased item or service is explicitly clear to both the buyer and the seller.

3   There are an adequate number of suppliers who are both willing and able to supply.

4   There is sufficient time for the buyer to prepare the invitation and for potential suppliers to produce a well-thought-out and documented bid.

5   It is possible for suppliers to estimate the costs involved with a high degree of precision.

6   It is not anticipated that changes will need to be made to the specification at a later date. Otherwise a supplier may bid low in order to get the contract and when 'locked in' to it make a larger profit from later alterations to the specification.

If these conditions exist then the lowest bid usually represents a fair and reasonable price. However, a buyer should not conduct the bidding process in a mechanical fashion. As with all price analysis and negotiation, common sense should be used and the resulting price compared with other benchmarks such as the price paid in the past for a similar piece of work.

Comparison with market prices
Where there are many suppliers of a product or service, competition and the laws of supply and demand usually result in a fair price. This is generally true if the product is a standard one. If there is any basis on which the product or service can be differentiated from competitors, then the supplier may charge, and get, a premium price. One role of the professional buyer is to question the need for the differentiated product and seek to get agreement to use a standard product which costs less but provides the same core functions.

Comparison with historic prices
Comparing the current price with that paid in the past for the same, or similar, item can give an indication of the reasonableness of the price. However, you must always question whether conditions have changed since the last purchase was made and if so, whether historic price is now a fair one to use for comparison purposes.

Target pricing
Target pricing is used when price analysis is impractical or does not allow the buyer to arrive at the conclusion that the price is reasonable. It can also be used to identify the major cost components of a purchase as a basis of working with suppliers on cost reduction projects.

The first step is to obtain a cost breakdown of the purchased item or service. Many buyers now require their suppliers to provide this as part of the tendering process or as part of the commitment to partnership sourcing. If we cannot obtain such a breakdown directly from the supplier, an alternative way is to produce our own using our in-house experts. This latter way of identifying the different elements of purchase cost is sometimes called reverse engineering. The resulting analysis should look something like this example.

		£
Direct material	20kg @ £6/kg	120
Less scrap	5%	6
Net direct material cost		114
Purchased components		107
Total material cost		221
Direct labour	3 hours @ £10/hour	30
Variable production costs		251
Fixed production costs		105
Other fixed costs		180
Total costs		536
Selling price		600
Profit		64 *or* 10.7%

We can then use our own knowledge, or that of our colleagues in engineering and production, to review whether these individual costs are fair.

Learning and experience curves

Researchers have shown that in some industries labour costs reduce as the total volume of production increases. In addition, they have shown that these costs reduce in a predictable manner. The relationship between costs and volume is called a learning curve.

A learning curve is usually described in terms of the percentage cost reduction achieved by each doubling of production. So, for example, a 30% learning curve means that costs reduce by 30% each time production is doubled. This is understandable, as we would expect the labour force to become more efficient and skilled at carrying out a complicated task the more times they do it.

Learning curve reductions relate to direct labour costs. In a similar way, total costs fall as volume increases due to organisational improvements brought about by management. Examples of this are material cost reduction through product redesign, and manufacturing efficiencies brought about by process improvements.

The importance of these concepts to the buyer is that they can be used as aids in target pricing analysis to judge whether current prices are fair, and also as a basis for agreeing future cost reduction targets.

Negotiations

As we have seen, the price that a seller ideally wants can be modified in a number of ways. The question for buyers is how to go about modifying the price to get it as low as possible, without affecting other considerations such as logistics costs and the quality of service needed.

One way is to use competitive tendering and to rely on competition to drive the price down. This is not always practical and does not necessarily get the best result.

Another way is to enter into a negotiation with selected suppliers. The hallmarks of a good negotiation are that it:

- Produces a result that is fair to both parties
- Is efficient in terms of the time taken and resources used to reach agreement
- Improves, or at least does not damage, the relationship between buyer and seller

Too often, however, a typical negotiation starts with the seller stating the price and conditions he or she wants, and then the buyer putting in a counterbid. The negotiation proceeds with each side conceding a little ground until a compromise is reached somewhere between the two opening positions.

The result can fail all three criteria for a good negotiation. If one of the parties is very much stronger than the other, their bargaining strength may have resulted in a contract which seriously undermines the financial stability of the other party. This is rarely an efficient process, as both parties may need to break off and consult other members of their organisation before agreeing. Also, it is easy for one or other of the parties to get locked into their bargaining position and for the whole process to become very confrontational. Concessions are then made in a spirit of bad will and the relationship can be severely and permanently damaged.

Successful long-term negotiations are what are commonly called 'win-win' negotiations in which both sides come out of the negotiating process feeling that they have got a good and fair result. There are several key steps to achieving a win-win negotiation.

First, separate the people from the problem. Negotiations become confrontational when one party believes that they are personally being attacked or criticised. We must make sure that both parties recognise and understand what business issue is being negotiated. We should put ourselves in the other person's shoes and understand their perception and needs. We should communicate clearly and be an active listener and should not while away the time whilst the other party is speaking by thinking of the next thing that we want to say.

Second, we must invent options for mutual gain, and use brainstorming techniques to evolve as many solutions as possible. We should not judge any idea prematurely, or search for a single answer, and we shouldn't ever think that 'solving their problem is their problem'; we need to work together to solve problems.

Third, we must insist on objective criteria. The realities of life are such that even when trying for a win-win solution, there will inevitably be times when the interests of the two parties clash: we want delivery tomorrow, the supplier wants next week. When this happens we must insist on objective criteria for determining the outcome, for example, what is the industry standard?

Summary

Today we have looked at one of the most crucial aspects of purchasing: determining the purchase price. The key considerations are:

- There can be significant costs other than the initial purchase price involved in acquiring and using a purchased item; it is the total cost that we must reduce not just the purchase price
- There are potentially many factors which can persuade the selling company to modify its initial asking price; we need to understand what these factors are, and where and how to apply them
- If we are to negotiate successfully we need to analyse prices
- If we want productive and effective long-term partnerships with suppliers we must employ win-win approaches to negotiations. This means being hard but fair in our dealings with suppliers and searching for solutions which benefit both sides

Special purchases

There are some categories of purchase that are different to the ones we have described so far. These are:

- Services
- Capital equipment
- Projects

Services

Every company needs a wide range of services to support its core activity. Examples are cleaning services, catering, advertising and promotions, maintenance of plant and equipment and consultancy.

In many instances, the potential impact of these services can far outweigh the cost of the service bought. Consequently, the relationship between the specification of what is required, selecting the supplier, pricing the contract and a satisfied end user is complex. Getting the balance right is a key task for the buyer.

Specifying what we want
Earlier in the week we saw the critical role that the specification plays in buying goods. This is equally true when buying services.

The specification for a service contract is often called a Statement of Requirements or SOR. In many companies, the responsibility for developing the SOR lies with the user. A good buyer can provide an invaluable service to the user by offering his or her knowledge and expertise in defining a SOR.

In some instances, it may even be beneficial to invite potential suppliers to assist in preparing the SOR. This has two advantages. First, it enables us to use the contractor's expertise and knowledge and ensure that we are not over- or underspecifying critical aspects of the service. Second, it allows the potential contractors to get a better understanding of our organisation and the level of effort that will be required to meet our expectations fully.

The first step in preparing the SOR is to investigate the objectives of the contract and any constraints that have to be taken into account. The key tasks are:

- Deciding on the budget, timescales and any other constraints which need to be taken into account
- Defining the responsibilities of the different parties involved. For example, who will provide the materials to be used in the contract?
- Defining the tasks to be accomplished and the sequence of events needed to meet the overall contract deadlines. The buyer should challenge any key tasks and objectives already identified by the user, using value analysis techniques
- Identifying any technical aspects, such as specifications

The next step is to document our requirements. The same considerations we looked at in preparing specifications

earlier in the week equally apply here. We must strike a balance between being clear as to what is needed and allowing the supplier sufficient scope to use his or her initiative to meet the terms of the SOR at lowest cost.

Selecting the supplier
Selecting suppliers to fulfil service contracts can be more subjective than in selecting suppliers of materials. The reason for this is that we are often buying a capability which is difficult to measure. For example, if we are running a chemical plant which operates 24 hours a day, we need a supplier of maintenance services to be able to respond quickly at any time of day or night, seven days a week, 52 weeks a year.

For this reason, a major factor when selecting suppliers of some key services may be the reputation of the supplier. This in itself may restrict our choice to a few suppliers, or even, in extreme cases, to just one.

The next step in the supplier selection process is to issue an invitation to tender, or ITT, to the shortlisted suppliers. When all the replies are received, the task of the buyer is to document the replies so that they can be compared on a like-for-like basis.

TENDERS

Pricing the contract

If there are many potential suppliers of the service, competition may be sufficient to make sure that we pay a fair price. However, in some instances, there may be few potential suppliers or even just one. In other cases, it may not be clear at the outset as to the extent of the service that will be needed during the life of the contract. Under these circumstances, a mixture of good negotiation skills and an appropriate form of contract is needed.

The types of contract available to us fall into three categories:

Fixed contracts are exactly what the name implies – the price is fixed at the start of the contract period. A firm fixed price contract is the most desirable as we will know exactly what we will be paying. However, some contracts extend over a long period and suppliers may be unwilling to face the risk of inflation in their costs. For these contracts, it may be fairer to build into the contract an agreed mechanism for increasing the contract price should the supplier's own costs increase by more than a certain amount.

Incentive contracts are more appropriate if there is a high degree of uncertainty about the effort needed to fulfil the contract or where the supplier can have an impact on costs through their own initiatives. Under these circumstances, a contract which acts as an incentive for the supplier to look at better and lower cost ways of performing the contract can be a benefit. An incentive contract usually has three components; a target price, a maximum price and a formula for sharing any cost reductions below the target price.

Cost-based contracts differ from incentive contracts in that all the risk is borne by the customer. They should only be used when it is not possible to use either of the two previous contract types, as there is no incentive for the supplier to keep costs and therefore prices down. The supplier is reimbursed for any allowable costs and in addition is paid a fee for carrying out the service.

Capital equipment

Capital purchases are those items which are used on a continuing basis, unlike, say, raw materials which are consumed within a short space of time. They are items such as computers, machine tools and fork-lift trucks.

It is important to get the purchase decision right first time, as the company will have to live with the consequences for many years. One strand of this decision-making process is to consider the whole-of-life costs of the purchase not just the initial purchase price. The cost of spare parts for maintaining and repairing a machine over its working life, for example, can be much greater than its purchase cost. Other costs include commissioning, training and the eventual disposal of the machine.

Another aspect is the operating characteristics of the purchase. This is, perhaps, the most critical consideration when selecting the supplier as seemingly identical items from different suppliers can behave quite differently in operation.

For all these reasons, capital buying is usually a team effort between the user, the buyer and finance. In addition, the size of the spend may require the purchase to undergo a formal vetting and approval process by the company's senior management and Board of Directors.

Projects

In many industries, new products require significant investment in design and development and can take many months to come to market. This is particularly the case in high technology industries, such as electronic equipment for defence applications, or in consumer markets where the unit price of the product is quite high, such as the automotive industry. The development of a new product is generally managed as a project.

It is not uncommon in these cases for 70% or more of the cost of the final product to be determined during the development phase. Buyers need to be involved at this early stage to make sure that purchases for the final design can be supplied at a cost which makes the new product competitive in the market-place.

Buyers can have an impact in three main areas of a project's development:

- Long-term supply market monitoring
- Project cost control
- Component cost control

Monitoring supply markets
The very nature of projects means that for key purchased items there are usually few capable suppliers, and the technology they use changes and evolves at a rapid rate. Just look at the specification of cars today compared even with five years ago. If we choose suppliers and technologies which are not up to date, we can suffer from a lack of competitiveness in our own markets.

- For the major components that we purchase, do we know where competing technologies are in their life cycle?
- Do we know what improvements in product performance our customers are demanding?
- Do we know what technical and commercial risks are associated with each technology?
- Do we know what new technological competencies we will need to develop with existing suppliers or source from new suppliers and when we will need them?
- Do we know what sort of relationship (partnership, alliance, co-development) we will need to develop with new suppliers?
- Do we know the volume of our future requirements and what this represents in terms of the size of the market?
- Do we know what barriers to entry or exit exist in the supply market?
- Do we know how costs behave in our supply markets?

The more 'no' answers we get to these questions, the more we need to improve our systems for gathering and analysing market intelligence. Buyers can play a key role in this 'technological scanning' process by monitoring the performance of existing suppliers, and by searching for and developing new suppliers.

Project cost control

We saw earlier in the week the way in which the specification of a purchase influences its cost. This is even more the case when buying for projects, as meeting the requirements of the user depends on sophisticated and expensive technology. We need to strike a balance between meeting the performance objectives of the product and controlling costs, so that we can meet the pricing objectives of marketing and still make a profit.

The buyer needs to have special training and experience for projects. In addition to the expected buying skills, he or she must be able to discuss the technological aspects of project buying with engineers and suppliers.

Many companies have achieved this by creating the role of Purchase Engineer. This person is usually an engineer by training who has been seconded to the purchasing department for a period to learn the skills of buying. The tasks for the Purchasing Engineer are then to:

- Involve key suppliers before technological solutions are chosen for the project to make sure the choices are the best ones
- Assess the supply risks for the purchase elements of the project and produce a risk management plan
- Ensure that the overall project plan incorporates deadlines and workloads for the major purchasing tasks (for example, definition control, bidding process, design and change management)
- Produce cost targets for the major purchased items based on the overall cost objectives for the project
- Initiate value analysis exercises for the major purchases
- Produce a control report which records planned and actual spend on purchases
- Monitor non-price factors for purchases, such as quality and lead times
- Estimate the cost impact of design changes for purchased items

Component cost control

In addition to managing the purchasing aspects of the total project, the Purchase Engineer is also responsible for the purchase of the individual parts and sub-assemblies. The cost and delivery objectives of these are determined by the overall project plan. The buyer's task is to source them from the supply market so as to meet these objectives.

The process for buying the parts and sub-assemblies has a lot in common with the processes used for service and capital buying.

The starting point is to prepare a specification which meets the technological requirements of the overall project, but provides sufficient flexibility for the supplier to be innovative and cost competitive.

The technological scanning process described earlier will have identified the potential sources of supply. These will fall in to one of two groups:

- Partnership suppliers who have been involved in the design and specification of the purchased item
- A pool of suppliers who will be invited to tender for the purchase

The process is then to negotiate contracts with the first group on a win-win basis or to issue invitations to tender the second group. Both of these were discussed earlier in the week.

Summary

There are some categories of purchase which need special treatment. These tend to be irregular or even one-off purchases such as services or capital equipment. In many cases we are buying a capability and not a product. It is critical that the specification of what we want to buy is clear and unambiguous.

Purchasing these items is usually done by a team rather than a single buyer. The buying role is to bring commercial expertise and supplier management skills to complement the technical specification skills of the other team members.

Performance measures and continuous improvement

Performance measures can be a powerful tool for motivating both buyers and suppliers to achieve our company aims and targets.

There is an old adage that says 'what gets measured gets done'. However, we must be very careful in setting performance measures, as they will determine the things that our buying department and suppliers see as priorities. This may work against what is best for the company overall.

For example, suppose we set a buyer a performance measure of processing 50 purchase orders a day. On one day, the buyer receives a purchase requisition for a product which is not a standard one. Should the buyer process the purchase order quickly in order to meet his or her target, or spend time on investigating potential sources, producing cost analyses and finding out whether there is a cheaper way of meeting the user's requirements?

There are several points we need to keep in mind when deciding on the most appropriate performance measure for a particular buyer or supplier.

- The activity must be simple to measure: if people do not understand how performance measures are calculated, they will not be motivated to improve
- The performance measure must be quantitative whenever possible. However, some activities will by their very nature be subjective. For example, if we select a supplier for his design excellence, we will want to measure whether or not that supplier is contributing to our product design. This can only be measured subjectively by asking the design team for their views
- The person being measured must see a correlation between improvement in the activity and an improvement in the performance measure
- There must be quick feedback on the effect of changes in the activity. The longer the gap between performance and feedback, the less likely it is that the person concerned will be able to take corrective action
- The activity being measured must be under that person's direct control

The key skill for the buyer is to select measures which will motivate both his or her external and internal teams to produce consistently world-class performance.

We saw earlier in the week that successful purchasing strategies are based on an understanding of the interrelationships between supply market complexity and the importance to us of the purchased item. We can use a similar approach to decide on the most appropriate performance measures, as shown in the diagram below.

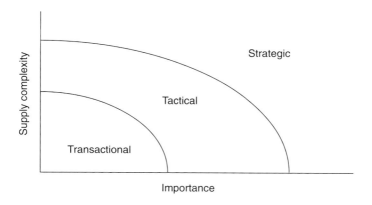

This diagram shows that there are three basic types of purchase each requiring different performance measures.

Transactional buying
These are products which are predominantly in the non-critical quadrant of the purchase portfolio. You will remember that our strategy for these products was to procure them as efficiently as possible. Our performance measures, therefore, need to focus on efficiency.

Efficiency measures are ones which look at the outputs of a process and compare them to the inputs. The more output we get for a given input, the more efficient is the process.

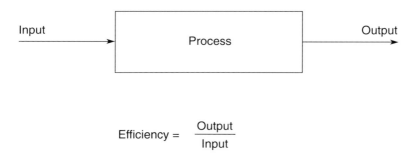

$$\text{Efficiency} = \frac{\text{Output}}{\text{Input}}$$

Typical inputs to transactional buying are:

- Cost (for example, overhead cost of the buying department)
- Headcount
- Systems

Typical outputs are:

- Volume of transactions, such as purchase orders
- Error rates
- Number of suppliers

Examples of performance measures which result from this are:

- Number of suppliers per buyer
- Error rate per hundred purchase orders
- Number of purchase requisitions per £ invested in systems

Applying this approach will give us a number of key ratios which measure the efficiency of our transaction buying processes. We can then monitor trends in the ratios and set targets for improvement. We can also compare the ratios for our business with those for others in the same industry using external surveys such as the ones published by CAPS.

Tactical buying
The key measures for this group should reflect the effectiveness of the buying process. There are many measures which can be used, and it is up to the buyer to decide which are the most appropriate for the specific needs of his or her own company.

The timing of deliveries is a key measure for most companies. The buyer's first responsibility is to support his or her company's line operations and ensure that supplies are available when needed. We can measure our effectiveness in doing this by monitoring:

- The percentage of overdue orders
- The percentage of stock-outs caused by late deliveries
- Number or production stoppages caused by later deliveries

- Actual delivery date compared with supplier's promised delivery date

Deliveries may be on time, but still cause problems because incorrect quantities were delivered. Therefore, we need some measure of the effectiveness of the process for getting the correct quantity. Typical measures are:

- Actual service level achieved by stock levels compared with target
- Delivery quantity compared to order quantity
- Stock-turns
- Report on stock surpluses due to overbuying
- Value of supplier stockholdings negotiated by the buyer
- Percentage of orders for which incorrect items were sent
- Percentage of orders for which split shipments were sent
- Quality of transportation used as measured by damaged shipments and incorrect documentation

A useful way to show measures such as delivery performance is with a graph:

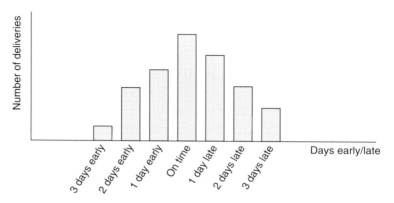

One chemical company uses this approach and measures each delivery from a supplier to see if it was on time in full. The answer is either yes or no. If the supplier gets five 'no's' out of 100 deliveries it is put on the 'sick list'. If it drops to 10 out of 100 that supplier is no longer used.

Another key measure of effectiveness is the quality of the items purchased. Some useful measures for this are:

- Percentage of items rejected
- Percentage of batches rejected
- Number of suppliers that have been certified by our quality team
- Number of suppliers using statistical process control techniques

Strategic purchases
You need to change the emphasis in performance measures to reflect the requirements of strategic purchases. The measures used for tactical buying change as follows:

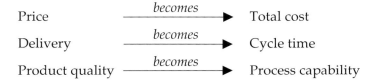

Total cost means all the costs associated with a purchase and not just the initial purchase price. This means, for example, the cost of stock holding to cater for long lead times, the cost of rework if the item fails in our production process, and the cost of warranties if our product fails when used by a customer and the failure is attributable to the purchased part.

These costs are often 'hidden' by accounting systems in the sense that they are not analysed and identified with a purchase, but are charged to accounts such as repair or warranty. We may find that changes are needed in our systems to allow us to calculate a true cost for a purchase.

Cycle time measures are aimed at the processes which affect our ability to meet our customer demand as quickly as possible. They cover areas such as the time to develop a new prototype, manufacturing process times, order processing times and delivery transit times. The shorter our supplier can makes these times, the more flexible and responsive we can become.

For transactional and tactical buying the most practical way of measuring quality is to choose suppliers who supply to a British Standard, or its equivalent, or have achieved some external certification such as BS 5750 (ISO 9000). We need to be more rigorous for strategic buying and take all precautions to make sure that we receive a quality product.

We can achieve this by assessing the supplier's production process and satisfying ourselves that it is capable of manufacturing to the tolerances that we require. Ongoing performance measures are then aimed at monitoring the process to make sure that it is performing to that quality. One way to do this is through statistical process control.

Performance measures for the buying department then revolve around the number of suppliers who have implemented statistical process control techniques and their continued adherence to them.

Setting targets

It is not enough to measure current performance. We need to set ourselves and our suppliers improvement targets. How do we do this so that the targets are challenging but still fair?

Brian Maskell, in his book *Performance Measurement for World-Class Manufacturing* (Productivity Press, 1991), discusses the concept of half lives. A study of a large number of companies undergoing improvement projects showed that the rates of improvement exhibited similar patterns even though the problems being addressed were different.

The conclusion drawn is that rates of improvement are consistent and can be expressed in terms of the time taken to halve the problem. For example, if it takes three months to halve the error rate in processing purchase orders from 4% to 2%, it will take another three months to halve the rate again to 1%.

The rule of thumb to use in setting targets is that for a situation which is under the direct control of one department or one supplier, the half life is typically three months. If we need cooperation to tackle the problem, the half life is typically nine months.

Competitive benchmarking

What is now generally called competitive benchmarking started at Xerox Corporation in 1979. Faced with mounting competition for its photocopier products, Xerox set about systematically comparing its operations with competitors with the aim of finding out what competitors did differently and better.

Robert C. Camp has documented the results of this process in his book *Benchmarking: The Search for Industry Best Practices that Lead to Superior Performance* (Milwaukee: Quality Press, OP).

The purpose of benchmarking is to find the most effective way for us to meet customer requirements and obtain customer satisfaction. Purchasing is one very important function in any company which contributes to these goals. Applying benchmarking concepts to purchasing can give us valuable insights into how to improve, and so is a powerful tool for setting performance measures.

Camp identifies a 10-step process for carrying out a successful benchmarking exercise. We have to:

1 Identify what is to be benchmarked. Purchasing, like any other business function, comprises different processes, each of which has an output. An example of this is the process for administering purchase orders which has a valid purchase order as its output. The key processes need to be identified which contribute to the company's mission of satisfying customers.

2 Decide the company or companies with whom we want to compare our processes. We will need to consider not only the leaders in our own industry, but also leading companies in other industries. After all, the aim is to outperform the best in our industry, not just achieve the same level as the best.

3 Decide how we will collect the data. This is not only hard data which measure the process being benchmarked, but also data on how best practice methods are performed.

4 Determine the current gap between our own process performance and that of the best practice leader. The gap will indicate the effort that we need to put into closing the gap.

5 Project future performance levels. Unless we take action, is the gap going to get bigger? What are the consequences of this for our company?

6 Communicate benchmark findings and get acceptance. Unless we demonstrate convincing findings based on hard data, we will not get the resources and support we need to make change happen.

7 Establish goals. As with all performance measures and targets, these need to be challenging but at the same time credible if they are to be motivating.

8 Develop action plans. The people who actually carry out the work tasks are usually in the best position to determine how the benchmark findings can be incorporated into current work practices. We must make sure we involve them.

9 Implement actions and measure progress.

10 Recalibrate benchmarks. Business life is not static. Competitors and best practice leaders in other industries

will also be taking steps to improve. We need to revisit benchmarks from time to time to make sure that the targets and plans we have put in place are still relevant.

Summary

Today we have looked at ways of assisting our efforts to become the best in our industry in the key purchasing processes. We looked at:

- Performance measures for transactional, tactical and strategic purchasing
- How to set targets which are challenging but at the same time motivating
- Benchmarking as a way to become the industry leader, and just as importantly, to stay there

The Business in a Week series

Doing Business in Europe in a Week

Finance for Non-Financial Managers in a Week

Introduction to Bookkeeping and Accounting in a Week

Succeeding at Interviews in a Week

Successful Appraisals in a Week

Successful Assertiveness in a Week

Successful Budgeting in a Week

Successful Business Writing in a Week

Successful Career Planning in a Week

Successful Computing for Business in a Week

Successful Customer Care in a Week

Successful Direct Mail in a Week

Successful Interviewing in a Week

Successful Leadership in a Week

Successful Market Research in a Week

Successful Marketing in a Week

Successful Meetings in a Week

Successful Mentoring in a Week

Successful Motivation in a Week

Successful Negotiating in a Week

Successful Presentation in a Week

Successful Public Relations in a Week

Successful Project Management in a Week

Successful Purchasing in a Week

Successful Selling in a Week

Successful Stress Management in a Week

Successful Time Management in a Week

Successful Training in a Week

Understanding BPR in a Week

Understanding Just in Time in a Week

Understanding Quality Management Standards in a Week

Understanding Total Quality Management in a Week

Understanding VAT in a Week